The Story of David and the Slingshot

Patricia A. Pingry

Illustrated by Katherine Wilson

A Word to Parents and Friends

This story is one of a series of biblical stories especially written, illustrated, and designed to explain a difficult concept in a gentle and simple manner.

Even the youngest child will understand the timeless lesson inherent in each bible story. Most of all, preschoolers, beginning readers, and older children will enjoy hearing and reading these exciting accounts of heroes from one of the oldest and most exciting books of all: the Holy Bible.

Ideals Publishing Corporation
Nashville, Tennessee

ISBN 0-8249-8180-4

In a faraway land, many, many years ago, there was a young boy named David. David was a shepherd. Each day, David took care of a flock of sheep. He fed the sheep. He made sure they had water to drink. And when a sheep got lost, David searched until he found it.

David kept his sheep safe from wild animals.
Sometimes a lion or bear came to steal a sheep. David
would take his slingshot and a stone and kill the wild
animal. David loved his sheep.

When the sheep were quiet, David would play his harp and sing. He sang many songs of thanksgiving and praise to God who protected him.

David had seven brothers. Three of his brothers were in the army with King Saul. One day, David's father asked David to take some bread to his brothers and see how they were. Early in the morning, David left his sheep with another shepherd and set out to find his brothers.

David found the army. It was preparing for battle against the Philistines. The Philistines had a giant on their side. He was nine feet tall and his name was Goliath. Goliath stepped out in front of the enemy line of soldiers. He yelled at King Saul's army. And the king's army ran back in fear.

     When David saw his brothers run back afraid,
David yelled, "Who is this soldier that he can frighten
God's army?"

     His brothers were angry that David saw their fear.
His brothers were afraid Goliath might hear David and
hurt them.

David wasn't afraid of Goliath. He turned to the other soldiers and said again, very loudly, "Who is this man who makes God's army run?" King Saul heard of David's talk and sent for him.

When David came before the king, he said, "Don't be afraid. I will fight the enemy!"

The king saw that David was only a boy, not old enough or strong enough to be a soldier. He told David that the giant had been fighting for years and no one had defeated him. But David told Saul how he had killed lions and bears and saved his sheep. He said, "My Lord has saved me from wild animals. He will save me from this enemy, too!"

To protect David from the giant, Saul gave David a coat of armor, a sword to wear, and a bronze helmet for his head. David thought all that metal was too heavy. He could not move his arms very well. He couldn't run. He couldn't even walk very well!

David took off the sword. He took off the helmet.
He took off the armor. He picked up his bag of stones
and the slingshot which had killed the lions and bears.
And he walked out to meet the enemy soldier.

Goliath saw the boy coming and laughed at him. He said, "Am I only a dog that you come after me with a stick and stones?"

But David said, "You come against me with a spear and a sword. But I come to fight you in the name of the Lord Almighty, the Living God, whose army you have defeated."

Goliath moved to attack David. David ran quickly toward the giant, reached into his bag for a round smooth stone, and slung it toward Goliath. It went straight and true and struck Goliath just above his nose, right in the center of his forehead. Goliath fell facedown on the ground. The shepherd boy had killed the giant.

From that moment on, David stayed with King Saul. When the king was upset, he sent for David to play his harp and sing. David sang many songs of thanksgiving and praise to God. And God protected David all the days of his life.